Amazing Words

Edited By Byron Tobolik

First published in Great Britain in 2021 by:

Young Writers
Remus House
Coltsfoot Drive
Peterborough
PE2 9BF
Telephone: 01733 890066
Website: www.youngwriters.co.uk

All Rights Reserved
Book Design by Davina Hopping
© Copyright Contributors 2021
Softback ISBN 978-1-80015-674-6

Printed and bound in the UK by BookPrintingUK
Website: www.bookprintinguk.com
YB0488C

Foreword

Young Writers began thirty years ago. Three decades, 360 months, 1560 weeks or 10,950 days (give a leap day or two!).

To put that into context, when Young Writers first started John Major was the UK's Prime Minister, mobile phones were the size of a brick, and the World Wide Web was just a single page, not yet available to the public.

A lot has changed since then, and Young Writers has been there every step of the way, helping young poets and authors to chronicle those changes across the years through their creative writing. From the rise of technology and social media, to the fall of animal populations across the globe, to changing attitudes, we've seen it all, and young writers from across the country and across the years have explored it all through the medium of poetry.

A lot of those poets are now grown up, and may have had children of their own who are now embarking on their own creative journey, exploring the world and their feelings through words, and in the process discovering not only their skill and creativity, but also themselves. That's pretty amazing, and definitely something to celebrate!

So we decided to celebrate the only way we know how – through poetry! We asked for poems on any theme and in any style, so this birthday book is filled with eclectic poems from a range of voices. What are you waiting for? Come on in and join the Big Poetry Party.

And here's to the next 30 years!

Contents

Independent Entries

Alanna Anish (13)	1
Andrada Ivascu	2
Lucy Perry (11)	6
Anushka Mukherjee (14)	8
Asmi Mathkar	10
Mahjabeen Mughal (14)	13
Keziah Kernal (13)	14
Maximilian Kufuor (9)	17
Isaac Chandler (18)	18
Lilly Robson (10)	21
Evie Hazell (15)	22
Urvashi Godhania (9)	25
Micah Frimpong-Boatey	26
Izza Kamil-Okedara (15)	28
Gabriela Stryjewska (13)	30
Julia Zmarzla (13)	32
Lauretta Wong (17)	34
Violetta Cheng (8)	36
Niamh Sharkey (14)	38
Libaan Siddiqui (11)	40
Jennifer Poulter (14)	42
Elizabeth Onikute (10)	44
Saumya Kulkarni (8)	46
Aiza Majeed (12)	48
Ipsa Bathla	50
Esther Onikute (10)	52
Vivienne Yassa (9)	54
Adelina Ahmetaj	56
Lily Dawes (11)	58
Abisha Jayan (13)	60
Calli-Mai Caulton (10)	62
Abisana Mohanathas (9)	64
Lazzaro Pasquariello (10)	66
Jessica Elizabeth Miller (14)	68
Monika Shinh	70
Fahira Mirza (14)	72
Shaheer Sami (13)	74
Ruthie Forsythe (8)	75
Catherine Thomas (12)	76
Megan Hawkins (12)	78
Rituparna Mishra (15)	79
Farwa Khan (15)	80
Maisie Severn (10)	81
Micah Forsythe (6)	82
Ali Ghazi (12)	84
Rebecca Morrison (8)	85
Patricia An (13)	86
Estella Thompson Oakley	88
Bethany Hoccom (13)	89
Joyce Chen (12)	90
Oskar Królak (13)	91
Elena Mason (9)	92
Hannah Marie Bignell (12)	93
John Segbefia	94
Jade Effemey (16)	95
Emily Hogg (16)	96
Kiera Ashton (16)	97
Ellie Jones (12)	98
Kavithan Davidprapakaran (8)	99
Nawal Ali (13)	100
Shaheera Kuchai (14)	101
Richard Chen (11)	102
Victor Uzoma (10)	103
Benjamin Doeteh (15)	104
Holly Hopkinson (12)	105
Daisy Blacklock (12)	106
Alicia Cocks	107
Jasmine Natasha Oakey (16)	108
Dhyan Amith (8)	109

Ava Maconachie (12)	110
Alesha Sami (6)	111
Aniqa Khan (9)	112
Amy Liddell	113
Elizabeth Hurley (9)	114
Deakon Marcus (10)	115
Elysia Miller (9)	116
Amelia Amirthaponkalan (8)	117
Natalia Szutenberg (9)	118
Charlie Nisbet (12)	119
Zoha Fathima (9)	120
Tariq Konkobo (11)	121
Kellsie Hindle (10)	122
Ramondeep Singh Gahir Gaidhu (12)	123
Michelle Alenoghena (8)	124
Jaspinder Singh Kaur (11)	125
Arabella Pasquariello (7)	126
Ivy Lucas (7) & Imogen Lucas (5)	127
Ezaan Ijaz (10)	128
Elizabeth Byrom (6)	129
Taaraz Siddiqui (6)	130
Amerie Anderson	131
Menaal Khan (8)	132
Arli Mohammed	133
Aqsa Kamran (5)	134
Penelope Pickup (7)	135
Sarah Uwadia (12)	136
Alfie Trout (8)	137
Fatimah Wahid (11)	138
Yousuf Kabir (5)	139
Rose Tobie (6)	140
Zara Mehta	141
Chidimma Mbah (7)	142
Hajrah Bibi (10)	143
Emmi John (14)	144
Aaron Thomas Hindle (9)	145
Henry Martin	146

Happy 30th Birthday

"**H** appy birthday!" you finally wake up to,
A nd breakfast in bed you happily munch through.
P erfectly dressed and helping by,
P utting up decorations and eyeing the cake with an impatient sigh.
Y earning for your friends to come with presents,

3 times bigger than last year's presents.
0 tails pinned correctly on the donkey so,
T he clown cheers things up with a show.
H appy birthday is sung while you,

B low the candles and make a wish that hopefully comes true.
I nto all mouths go,
R olls and pizzas and jellies and so and so.
T hen the time comes for you to make sure your friends,
H ave a party bag as the party sadly ends.
D irty dishes and rubbish needing clearing but you,
A re so exhausted that you can't move like a tight screw.
Y ou yawn but you don't fail to begin: "When is my next b'day?"

Alanna Anish (13)

Captain Seas

Poor, poor Captain Seas,
He fell and landed in a shrub of bees,
He started to cry, "Please, please, Almighty Lord!
Send me back to my ship aboard!"

The bees stung like mad,
And he thought it hurt really, really bad,
There he sat on the dirt throne,
While the bees almost broke his bones.

There were so many rashes on his face,
That he could not see to tie his shoelace,
He tried to walk, he tried to run,
Just to get on the ship to eat a syrup bun.

Poor, poor Captain Seas,
One day, he wanted to eat frozen peas,
He tried to swim in the ocean,
But forgot his magical potion.

The magic potion helped him float,
It's just like how he fell in the water off the boat,
He would lay there silent and still,
Not caring to help his teammate Pirate Bill.

So, of course, he nearly drowned at the bottom,
But he was helped by Pirate Cotton,
He spoke, "Thank you very much for saving me!
You are as kind as God can be!"

Poor, poor Captain Seas,
Always saying the word please,
Because he is really, really clumsy,
The same as his friend Pirate Bumsy.

His clumsy actions stopped him from doing stuff,
Like being a history buff,
He would discover fossils and more,
Whilst trying to pull the ship's core.

Obviously, that did not end well,
And he began to ring the bell,
Pulling really hard like how they play guitars in a band,
He didn't notice the puddle of quicksand.

He fell in whilst trying to pull hard,
And he was saved by Captain Nard,
He spoke, "Thank you very much for saving me!
You are as kind as God can be!"

Poor, poor Captain Seas,
Landed in a shrub of bees,
Tried to eat frozen peas,
He kept saying the word please.

Enough was enough for him,
And it was also enough for Captain Tim,
He decided not to be clumsy anymore,
And buy a magical potion from a magical store.

It cost about 20,000 gold coins,
And he bought the potion from an isle named Boys,
He drank it really, really fast,
And he felt like he was in the past.

He started seeing unicorns dancing like mad,
And he was really, really sad,
Because he could not dance with them,
While the unicorn shouted, "Good afternoon, Ma'am!"

"What? I'm not a ma'am!" he spoke,
As the unicorn pulled out a purple bloke,
"Your clumsiness will now go away because of me!
So remember to be as careful as you can be!"

The unicorn spread the magic around Captain Seas,
And suddenly, he forgot about being stung by bees,
And eating frozen peas,
And always saying the word please.

He spoke, "Thank you, thank you, magic store!"
Because he knew he wouldn't be clumsy anymore,
Thinking about how many things he could do now,
Things that he didn't know how.

Andrada Ivascu

The Forest Is On Fire

Oculto the ocelot awoke with an ear-splitting boom,
He sprinted out of the cave as the flowers began to bloom,
A crackling fire set the trees ablaze,
Oculto gazed at the crackling amaze,
He'd never seen the flames before.
"My forest is on fire!" Oculto swore.

He brushed past flowers and sprinted past the trees,
He halted at a buzzing sound and found a hive of bees.
"What is going on?" he said,
With a concerned expression on his ferocious head.
"The furless apes are roaming our land!
Burning our forest, they don't understand!
We'll have nowhere to live! Nowhere to hide!
What's a world where animals have died?"
The bee warned as she buzzed with a sigh,
Suddenly, a squawk sounded from up high.

A toucan perched on a low twig in a tree.
"What's going on? Those apes are frightening me!"
The toucan chirped sorrowfully at the cat,
They silently waited, they sat and they sat.

A tree frog approached, hopping with sadness.
"We are going to run!" Oculto said with a hint of gladness,
The animals cantered far and wide,
Nowhere to run, nowhere to hide,
The bee buzzed and the frog let out a croak,
Their beautiful habitat was nothing but smoke,
All was silent, all was dead,
The crackle and sizzle still played in their head,
Wherever they gazed, looked and peeped.
"There is no green!" the toucan shrieked.

"Our home is destroyed!" the frog whined.
"All apes are nice! All apes are kind!
Why don't these furless ones live as one?"
All was dark, no moon, no sun,
The forest was a pile of crackling ash,
All trees were gone, except one with a gash,
A tall tree stood tall and proud,
The furless apes were unfriendly and loud,
Have you ever met an animal this mean?
"Beware of these apes!"
Oculto licked himself clean.

Lucy Perry (11)

The World Without Adults

"Ladies and gentlemen, this is the world without adults,
Some call it the world of fun, others call it the world of mayhem,
But I guarantee, this heritage site is a real gem!
Now, let us begin our walk through the city,
Observe the gingerbread buildings; an idea most witty!
To your right, we now pass some primary schools,
I should inform you, our education system has few rules;
Exams are prohibited by law, as is homework,
School is optional, like any form of work-
Sir, please! Watch where you are going...
You may step into a waste zone without knowing.
You see, none of the kids here like to tidy up and waste starts to pile,
So we hide the rubbish in waste zones," she explained with a smile.
"Our city is the most eco-friendly of its kind,
Mainly due to the way our transportation is designed.
We use life-sized wind-up trains, buses, and planes to fly,
And that is how we bid our carbon emissions goodbye!
Not a single piece of plastic is used,
Our main material is candy and chocolate fused."

"If I may interrupt, I have some questions, Miss Tour Guide."
"I can answer any questions you have," she answered with pride.
"Isn't it dangerous to have candy buildings, as they may collapse?
Or wind-up aeroplanes if they crash, perhaps?
Once the kids in your city grow up, where do they move?
To the normal world, where you came from... what exactly are you trying to prove?
How do they survive out there if they aren't educated?"
"I don't know. Are you trying to insult us?" she asked irritated,
"All I'm saying is that the world without adults needs adults, and that is a fact,
Children need grown-ups, your city is just an act!
A world without adults is a fun thought, at first,
But it would actually be a disaster at its worst!"
The flustered girl did not know how to reply.
"Ladies and gentlemen, I think it is time we said goodbye,
I do hope you enjoyed your visit to the world without adults."

Anushka Mukherjee (14)

The Seasons

Clear skies spread above me,
While damp grass grazes my bare feet
The leaves fall down, crunching slightly,
As the golden sun shines in a haze.

The crackling fire burns
As the smell of hot coffee wafts towards me.
Soft pattering of rain is heard,
While warm sweaters engulf me.

Reds, golds, oranges and browns swirl around me,
The faint smell of apple and cedarwood can be felt,
Until All Hallows' Eve,
When soft music is replaced with eerie sounds.

Suddenly, a sharp gust of wind is felt,
As stormy clouds shroud the sun.
The first snowflakes drop silently,
As the darkness sets in.

Lights strung up,
As the hearth emanates warmth,
Contrasting with the gloom outside,
And matching the excitement within.

As the bells toll,
The bedazzled tree sparkles,
And children are quaking in anticipation,
For Christmastime has come.

But eventually, the snow melts,
As fresh blossoms peek out of the damp ground,
Green leaves grow steadily,
As the sun returns from its slumber.

Picnic blankets laid out,
In small crevices of woodland,
Speckled with light from the sun through the trees,
Enchanted by the aroma of the flowers.

Days grow longer,
The air gets warmer,
Anticipation lurks everywhere,
For the excitement of summer.

Like a flash, the summer sun begins to shine,
The days pass by in a haze of fun,
The holidays begin, they bring with them the unquenchable bubble of joy,
As water fights and beach days commence.

Ice cream sundaes all around,
Bedazzled with sprinkles and multicoloured sauces,
Enjoyed in the shade of an oak tree,
Protecting me from the sweltering heat.

Golden sunsets end the day,
A myriad of colours, swirled with a subtle glow,
Warm, cloudless, moonlit nights,
Peppered with stars.

The seasons change,
Each one brings a new delight,
As we travel through the year,
A truly marvellous journey.

Asmi Mathkar

Builders Of Misery

Through our blind eyes, we cannot see;
In every blink, our minds condemn,
As to what our future Earth could be.
What deceiving trap have we been in then?
Through every church bell that calls,
Ancient books bring forth a demonic presence,
That lure us into unconsciousness,
The lords and ladies disdain the lower,
Oblivious that to the aboding evil, they are peasants.
Through every fire that sparks,
That lets out the shadows of bemoaning ghosts.
Though every scientist's mark;
We still cannot see.
Through every wave that eats away,
Leaving putrefied bones of cities.
Through every cry of man today,
That shows our slavery.
We still cannot see.
The thing that holds the most beauty,
That comes in many forms,
Traps the human eye with numeric terms.
It's the very thing that kills, but silently does it,
Leaving us blind.
We are the builders of misery.

Mahjabeen Mughal (14)

Vision

Vision,
The word for being able to see,
To see around us,
Or be able to use our imagination,
To imagine the world in a way,
Only we are able to do.

People's minds work in different ways,
Some might see a utopia,
The perfect world,
With no discrimination or hate,
Or a world where we need not worry
About our planet's health,
A world where pollution is not destroying
Us and the Earth.

Others imagine a dystopia,
A world full of hate, greed and desire,
Where people only care about themselves,
And places like care homes for the elderly,
And things like hospitals and emergency services,
Never exist.

Everyone has a vision,
Of what their dream world would be,
Of what they imagine,
The modern world to be.

Some let their imagination,
Run wild and free,
Others keep it inside the box,
And limit themselves to their eyes,
And their perspectives,
Ignoring what they could see,
If they just opened up.

The door to your vision,
Is always wide open,
Full of utopias and dystopias,
Fulls of dreams and perspectives,
And lots of other stuff,
Which is bound to change.

My vision,
Is what I see,
And no one can change it,
It is unique to me,
And only for me.

Vision,
Vision is a complex thing,
With very many layers,
Vision is something that is not to be understood,
Instead,
It is to be explored,
Letting our dreams run wild,
And finding the full potential of,
Our vision.

Keziah Kernal (13)

Marvin

This is my pet called Marvin.
He swims in my fish tank like an ordinary fish,
But when I go to school, he opens a secret hatch!
He goes inside and hacks computers,
With robot hands that are attached to him.
There was a robber fish in the city.
It was Marvin's evil brother, Marlin.
He had a secret hatch too
And when Marlin pressed a red button,
It caused chaos around the world.
Marvin knew that Marlin liked fries and lies,
But he hated pies.
One day, when I went out,
Marvin went inside his hatch and killed Marlin
By pressing a green button, but he had to lean.
On the eighth of April 2021,
Marvin lost one eye and struggled to survive.
Unfortunately, he passed away and left me devastated.
I miss him so much.

Maximilian Kufuor (9)

Moonlight

Arms, outspread as if an effigy,
Loitering amongst the reeds,
The lake reflects the light of the moon,
To sing the song of the perigee-syzygy.

Arms carrying the weight of my heart
Begone are the euphoric days
Full of compunction is my core
Done is my journey, establish the fraise.

Brow ahead; the hill casts a shadow,
Dew, the only sign of life
Rose dead. Reflects me
Too glum, too grim to live.

Meads possess no zeal of life,
Child born.
Light and innocent
Wildness submerged by the veil of youth.

Head above the ground, yet not breathing
Zoned into non-existence.
Love hammered a hole within me
Moonlight, the only constant presence.

Steed long-forgotten, no longer needed
Zoned out of chivalry.
Sing the song she used to sing,
The song ingrained within me.

Sweet music, no longer heard
Dew continues to fall.
Said, "Je t'aime."
True, those words will never be stirred.

Elfin Grot, the place I first saw her.
Sore, to see that place again
Eyes, tearful to see that sight
Four days, here I have spent

Asleep, not me, unbeknownst what would
Betide. Amongst the reeds, in my reverie,
Dreamt her face beside me
Side by side, our bodies touch.

Too quick, it ends.
All the solitude returns.
Merci was she, a
Thrall to my guilt, I have become.

Gloam brings yet more darkness
Wide expanses, overarching
Here, there, everywhere,
From side to side, surrounding.

Here, I lie in wait. Blighted.
Loitering in the forgotten hollow,
The lake entices me, bottomless, mighty,
Sing to me, my love, we shall soon be reunited.

Isaac Chandler (18)

Wolves

The wolf catches its prey,
And rips, tears, shreds,
The flesh from its enemy.
The prey squeals for help,
As its skin gets torn to pieces.
As the next victim approached,
The wolf ran fast like a cheetah in a pack.
The deer galloped away,
As fast as it possibly could.
Dangerously, the wolf began to catch the innocent deer.
The deer was now petrified,
Fearing for its own life.
Catching the deer,
He once again viciously tore the deer to pieces.
The deer watched its sister get eaten,
He felt sick and useless,
Like he couldn't stop the mean wolf.
A human onlooker hid in the dark,
Shadow of doom,
As the wolf slowly approached.
The wolf was terrified of the human,
Had the tables finally turned?

Lilly Robson (10)

So Incredibly Exciting

I cannot wait,
To love every part of what I do,
To listen to the wind whisper my fate.

To laugh at jokes that aren't funny,
At 1am in a rooftop bar.
To see all that should be seen.
The wonders, adventures, jewels of the Earth.
To travel to the darkest unfinished corners.

I can't wait to be brave,
To inspire,
To try,
To fail,
To learn from my mistakes,
To succeed in as many ways as I can.

To talk about things I love with people that will listen.
To cry at the little things,
And the things that hurt me most.
Because I know I'll overcome them.

I can't wait to be surprised and truly not expect it.
To see pictures from 15 years ago,
That will embarrass me,
But they make life so much more enticing.

To buy my first house,
Drive a car, own a pet,
Buy furniture,
Build my forever home.

To go to a restaurant alone,
And buy myself a drink.
To make a difference in the world,
No matter how small or big.

I can't wait to meet a stranger,
And learn everything about them,
Then never see them again.

I can't wait to endlessly watch the stars,
Until my eyes go star-shaped,
With rainbows beaming from my face.

I can't wait for secret notes,
Real phone calls lasting hours.
To scream until the mountains crumble,
And wake up to the sun pouring through my curtains.

I can't wait to meet that stranger,
10 years later on with so much to say.
I can't wait to grow old,
And stop worrying about what others think.

I cannot wait.
But I will,
Because it makes it so incredibly exciting.

Evie Hazell (15)

Nature's Problem

I'm afraid to say, I've swallowed an apple seed,
And now it's growing its roots inside my belly.
I believe that the trunk will run straight up through me,
Until I have a wooden spine and ribs of solid oak.
I think the seed will grow,
And make branches in my lungs,
Till it pokes holes in the chambers of my heart.
I'll become a common topiary,
A little sapling amongst others,
Soon, leaves and blossom will sprout from my nose.
The doctor says not to snack on soil if I can help it,
But Mummy laughed, so I think there is no proper cure.
I cried in the car as we turned from the junction,
And she turned to me and said -
That we'd go around and around,
Until my pip falls out and I'm just a little pot again.

Urvashi Godhania (9)

Legends Never Die

Let me pause for a minute,
Caught your hearts whilst catching digits,
In a no hope environment,
I can only imagine how enlightening it feels to say you did it,
Now you've done it,
Sliding into your comfort zone like McFlurries,
But your face is screaming: "I'm loving it."
They don't know behind the scenes like when times were troubling,
Now you're the diamond in the dirt that everyone's discovering.
Oh, so life has changed,
From the projects to a microphone and a stage.
In a league of your own where your expression adds flavour,
'Cos you're giving them a taste of what hard work and pain is.
No fugazi, a lot of setbacks that you trained your mind for,
Expect the unexpected.
I'ma grind so hard that they have no choice but to respect this.
All my enemies have their agendas,
But I don't reside with the small-minded because ignorance is what they resemble.

They only grind for designer,
I'm grinding to guide a way and that's why they don't like us,
Or maybe because they ain't like us.
Every result I get from taking a risk, I drop a tear,
They don't take risks and that's why they live in fear.
Supreme doesn't make you superior,
When you looking at the mirror.
Due to all my fallen soldiers, I look to the sky,
I live life, if they don't like the truth, that's why they live a lie.
That's why I'm dying to live and living to die,
Legends never die.

Micah Frimpong-Boatey

Ambush

The clouds gather in the Heavens
Speaking of matters unbeknownst to
The mortal beings which scamper below.
Yet the sudden darkening of the sky
Takes them by surprise
And from therein swarm legions of snow

Each soldier intricately sculpted
by the fine workmanship of God himself
If you were to see them from afar, they would appear
as a single, solitary body,
Radiating terror to those who dare approach.
Yet, if you were to look up close, you would see
each fragile flake floating like a fluorescent feather
eagerly waiting to touch the ground.

The mighty army takes over the land
In a rapid expansion gone out of hand
Seizing every rooftop, blade of grass and startled hair
At a speed to which no Napoleon, Caesar, nor
Rashidun could compare.

But

It takes but a few days for the tides to turn
As the sun rises in all its glory
And sends its battalions - each soldier a blinding ray
Bearing proudly the banner of day
Invading - the white mass is taken by surprise
Liberating - the animals open their eyes
Recompensating - the cold force slowly dies
And sinks deep into the ground below

The clouds disperse
And the mortals are unaware
Of when next they will be ambushed by snow.

Izza Kamil-Okedara (15)

How Special Can Birthdays Be?

"Happy 30th birthday!" they all screamed!
It is my dad's birthday today,
He's very special to me, but is also my biggest fan.
I once got published in a book made by Young Writers and he was so thrilled.
He always encouraged me to write more and enjoy myself, so I kind of made it my favourite thing;
Journaling, screenwriting, song lyrics and writing short stories, but I never got around to sharing them.
I never knew why, but I think it's because I would get less motivated if I didn't win.
It was my birthday a couple of weeks ago,
I told myself I would finally find what I wanted to do in the future and now look at me, I'm living in my own mess, still worried about other people's opinions.
Birthdays are a way to reflect on your past and not to script out the next year of your life.
I need to concentrate on accepting myself as the young, intelligent human being I am and I need to show myself that I can do it and not just tell myself to be perfect, better and force myself to fit in.
So happy birthday Dad, Cara Delevingne, Mario Balotelli, Khris Middleton because they are successful;

I want to be like them.
Team leader, model, footballer or basketball player,
Whatever it is!
A new year for them and a new chapter for me.

Gabriela Stryjewska (13)

The Stranger

"Have you ever seen this man?
He's wanted and on the run,
He's not from around here,
But there are some bad things he's done.

His eyes are sunken in,
His moves seem tired and slow,
He looks quite old and keeps to himself,
And dips his chin down low.

But don't let this mislead you,
This man can cause some harm.
If you spot him, please inform us,
And try to stay calm."

That's what the policeman said,
Unknowing of the danger
And oblivious to the fact
That he was talking to the wanted stranger.

But this stranger just smiled,
Tipped his hat and walked away.
He turned into a dim alley
That smelt of rot and decay.

The man stepped through a door,
His face twisted into a grin.
He straightened his back and stretched his arms
Then started to peel off his skin.

But it wasn't his skin.
It was one he decided to borrow
From the young man who used to live down the street
His eyes were always full of sorrow...

He laid the shed skin
Carelessly on the ground.
Then he looked at his watch,
Saw the hour and frowned.

The time was already up;
He'd barely had his fun,
But when the darkness arrived
He was the one who would have to run.

You see, even the monsters aren't fearless
As there is always something worse,
And if you aren't afraid of anything,
That means the Devil has laid his curse.

Julia Zmarzla (13)

Reading Is Such An Unhealthy Thing To Do

Reading is such an unhealthy thing to do.
The more you read, the more you stray from reality.
The fictional world is an escape but oh, just how addicted it makes you.
There's this line where you're inspired by all sorts of creativity and imagination,
But the moment you pass it, there's nowhere to return to.

It's the worst with romance, fantasy.
You either become the hopeless romantic or the pessimist,
Dead on the inside, miserably.
All the hope and love you thought you'd learnt were just too good to exist.
It's the moment you realised fiction is not it,
The moment you stopped thinking
Whether you're more hopeful after each read
Or just more and really dead before sleep.

I, myself, never fantasise about finding love.
Take it easy,
They say.

Such a pity,
They say.
It'll be a truck when it hits,
They also say.
But deep down, it's me subconsciously refusing to commit and counting the days.
It is obviously my problem,
But I'm used to blaming the books,
The happiness they give and the false hope they preach.
Such a funny thing to be into -
Books.
When really, you're only happiest before you get addicted to -
Books.
Keep it to two a year and look,
You're fine! There's hope.

Lauretta Wong (17)

Birthday Party Vision

A birthday party, such fun it'll be
B alloons, dancing and cake for me
C ookies and cream, a wonderful dream
D oughnuts, grapes and mango ice cream
E ager friends all crowded around me
F antastic attention that'll be
G orgeous dresses that sparkle and shine
H andsome suits down the boy's spine
I 'll be crowded with presents and dancing with joy
J igging with glee at my marvellous new toy
K ing of the kingdom, that's how I'll feel
L ittle knowing that that isn't real
M any wonders that day, I'm sure will come true
N ot any chores for that day, in my view
O nly the good stuff that'll be left behind
P resents in wrappers are the images in my mind
Q uartz crystals and emeralds fit for a queen
R idiculously large, all shiny and clean
S ophisticated riddles I'll tell my friends
T errific laughter that never ends
U nder piles of books, I will be seen
V ery lost in a tale of kings and queens
W ondrous birthday, come soon the day
X mas is nothing compared to that day

Y es, I wish it would come soon
Z oom forward to my birthday, month before June.

Violetta Cheng (8)

What Makes Me Happy

What makes me happy is cold mornings on the way to school,
Laughing and chatting loudly with red noses being blown,
The thought of Christmas getting closer,
So the countdown begins.

Snow falls onto the ground while we watch from the classroom windows,
A voice telling us, "Get back to work!" and "It's like you've never seen snow before!"
But the classical movies still play when we're done.

The shops have queues right out the door,
Everyone thinking about the presents and who they are for,
Joy in the form of paper and a ribbon being torn open and a hug being given.

Cookies and milk sitting by the fireplace shadowed by expectant stockings,
Restless sleep and looking over your shoulder in case you spot someone special,
A jingle here, a bell there, a big white beard must be working hard this year.

What makes me happy?
What makes me happy is walking downstairs together into a dimly lit living room,
Where gifts for everyone lie waiting to be opened,
The shouts of delight and smiles all around.

What makes me happy is not the gifts at Christmas,
It's the feeling of being close.

Niamh Sharkey (14)

A Walk Down Ambition And Aspiration Street

From the fleeting glimpses of completing primary school,
Dreaming to be a footballer or even a scientist, looking like a fool,
Strolling through my years, at my limits with exams,
Passing with flying colours; going to Harvard or Oxford,
Praise and applause abound as awards and degrees fly inbound,
Aspiring to be all I can be with the needy all around,
Walking out of the gate once more, greeted with a joyous frenzy,
To be what I wished all those eras ago.
Equipped with knowledge and passion to fulfil my everlasting dream,
Setting off into the big, wide world with a wide beam,
Being elected as Prime Minister,
Signalling Britain from the depths of the ocean to the limits of the galaxy.
Showering the world with my utter brilliance,
To achieve the lifelong passion of mine,
Curing the world of contagious disease,
A Nobel Prize and knighthood, if you please,
Providing my family with a mansion and a Bentley,

Stepping down from my great and pristine-clear legacy,
Trying and struggling to live to a grand old age,
So others can be inspired and follow my lifelong passion.

Libaan Siddiqui (11)

One Day, We Will Reunite

One day, we will reunite,
Everything is just colourless, black and white.
Darkness fell, everyone draped in black,
No one, not one person could bear to smile,
Each person filled with emptiness, a blank space.
No one's face completely dry,
Everyone drenched in their own emotional reflexes.

Stood. Nothing could be seen, only white.
But then, a figure. Recognisable, known so well,
The figure for whom the sorrowful day had been for.
The figure held a white rose,
It spoke: "Do not worry, for one day we will reunite."

The white rose of death,
And then the darkness lifted.
Smiles were drawn for the sweet, sweet memories of whom the white rose took,
But then darkness fell again,
For the next eight weeks of drowning,
Drowning in emotion and uncontainable sorrow,

But then in those moments of suffering,
Just remember... Remember,
When the time is right,

The white rose will come for you too...
One day, we will reunite...
Then finally, you will be reunited,
And forevermore, you will live in a field of white roses.

Jennifer Poulter (14)

Love Is Dangerous

Write me down in history, but I will still rise
This is the story of my life
Just like the moon and the sun
They shine brightly just like my best friend did
It all started when I had a dream
A shadow came to me and said:
This is how I leave you
But I promise I'll be there
No matter what
That might have shot me down
That may have cut me down
That may have killed me
But I still had hope
My mom gave birth
To a beautiful girl
Just like the stars
She smiled, saying:
Inaya, that's what they call me
I will never ever leave you
But little did I know
Something was about to break me down
Something was about to kill me
My baby sister was gone
Just before my eyes

Why did I feel like God wasn't by my side?
Why did I feel alone?
Wasn't I good enough?
But after that, something happened
I rose up
I rose up like the dead
People wanted to bow their heads at me
But that wasn't happening.

Elizabeth Onikute (10)

Pegasi

Pegasi jump on clouds which makes them very proud.
Pegasi love rainbows and they've got good aim, you know.
I know that's weird, but it's true, and I know there's a place for you.
Pegasi love flying up high with a rainbow mane and glitter by their side.
Pegasi are bright which makes me fill up with light.
Pegasi have vanilla white wings that are as precious as diamond rings.

Pegasi are milky white like the moon at night.
I hope I have a magical ride that fills me up with pride.
As the birds twitter, Pegasi glitter which makes me flitter.
Pegasi shine with light until they are bright.
Pegasi have magic much better than you know
And they'll help you with which way to go.

Their wings have such a magnificent glow
As the water in the rivers flows.
The rainbow in their mane glows
As butterflies fly and go.
As the Pegasi fly
They look as beautiful as the birds in the sky.

Pegasi are my favourite creatures
And now you know its real nature.

Saumya Kulkarni (8)

Jealousy

My name is Aiza,
This is my poem,
My hopes for the future.

But there's one thing that has interrupted me,
Interrupted me for years and years on end.

The world wouldn't have life without it,
But when it's natural,
Or when it's pure envy,
It can be daunting.

The hatred that sprouts amongst it,
Breaking barriers of our lives,
Making the Earth dead,
Slowly killing us inside.

Is it the glare someone gives,
Or the fire inside?
Is it the sign they give,
Or letting sadness collide?

It hurts inside,
But you wanna show,
The other story.
Letting it take over,

Making you think life is just all
'Happily ever after'.

But back to the purpose
Of this poem,
My name is Aiza
And my hope for the future
Is to have a world without one thing,
Just one thing,
Jealousy.

Aiza Majeed (12)

Happy Birthday Young Writers

Poems, stories, sagas and tales
Young writers encourage
Many to write in different forms
And styles with courage.

This poem celebrates 30 years
Of them being an inspiration
They helped young kids
Expand their imagination.

Many competitions
And exciting events too
Chances to get work published
Chances for everyone, me and you

Young Writers was the platform
Which inspired many authors
They got a book published
And were surrounded by many more offers.

Happy birthday Young Writers
I hope you continue to inspire
Dreams and creations of
Many young people who aspire.

You are a supportive source of inspiration.
In which, what kids see are
A range of exciting themes and competitions
To help them expand their ideas.

Imagine! to Spine-Chillers
Silly School Trips to An Acrostic for You
Every competition you have done
Have encouraged another two.

Thank you, Young Writers
For bringing on the fun
For helping many to write
And by saying this, my poem is done.

Ipsa Bathla

Love Is Lonely

It all started when I imagined,
When I closed my eyes to be
Able to open my future.

Nowhere to go and no place to call home,
Then one night, my aunt had a baby.
I saw a baby with the brightest eyes,
He came to me with the sweetest smile.
Told me he wanted to talk for a while,
He said: "Baby Lolo, that's what they call me."
I promised him that he'd never be lonely.

I loved him dearly,
More and more, every second he was with me.
I held him so gently,
Then tears began to pour,
Because I knew by the end of the day,
I wouldn't have him anymore.
I'd have done anything to keep him out of harm's way,
But that didn't stop God's will,
I still lost a baby that day.
In my arms, he died.
How could I be so lost,
In a place I knew so well?
How could I be so broken,

In a family so together?
How could I be so lonely,
Surrounded by so many?
How could I be so unhappy,
Surrounded by so much beauty?
How could I be me?

Esther Onikute (10)

A Peculiar Party

I was thinking of having a party,
But not an ordinary party, a big party.

First, who shall I invite?
Hmmm, maybe the peculiar pets like:
Super hot sausage dog,
Fluffy the cat saving the day,
Flexible giraffe,
Raccoon the rock star,
Gilbert the clown,
Archie Button the chatterbox,
Bubba the boss,
Elvis the dancing tortoise,
I think I have everybody.

The party is tonight,
Everybody is excited.
I open my door, waiting...
Finally, they're here!
First in line is Raccoon the rock star,
He is ready to rock.
Next, Archie Button the chatterbox,
He likes to ask questions.
Elvis the dancing tortoise,
Then Bubba the boss,

Then Flexible giraffe,
Fluffy the cat saving the day,
And Super hot sausage dog
And Gilbert the clown.
We're ready to dance on the dance floor,
Bubba is doing her baby yoga.

Vivienne Yassa (9)

My First Year At Hogwarts

It's the start of the school year,
And everyone boards the train,
Off to Hogwarts we go,
I'm so excited, I could easily pop a vein.

I'm elated, yet nervous,
And my tummy has become an acrobat,
It's time for the sorting ceremony,
And I sit under the Sorting Hat.

I head up to my dorm,
So I can start to unpack,
On my way there, I'm startled by an owl passing by,
And I fall down the marble staircase with a big *whack!*

It's the first learning day,
And I wear my brand-new cape,
Professor McGonagall is teaching transfiguration,
And I turn the cape into a sweet, juicy grape.

Time flies by and now it's time to announce the Triwizard champions,
The title-holder for Hogwarts is me,
When I walk through the crowd,
I feel a feeling of gratification and glee.

It's time for the end of year exams,
And of course, I did well,
But now it's time to go,
Until next year Hogwarts, goodbye and farewell.

Adelina Ahmetaj

When I Am Older

When I am older, I want to be a scientist,
I want to be able to blow up the lab,
Experiment with chemicals,
And most of all, help people with my discoveries.

When I am older, I want to be a veterinarian,
I want to help animals,
Even if they are neglected and hurt,
I want to give every animal a chance to live.

When I am older, I want to be a police officer,
I want to keep people safe,
Investigate the crime of the missing cookie,
And make people pay for their crimes.

When I am older, I want to be a baker,
I want to make people smile,
Bake for every occasion,
And most of all, see children tapping on the window for cake!

When I am older, I want to be a nurse,
I want to help people,
I want to heal the sore wounds,
And see people walk again.

But most of all,
When I am older, I want to be an engineer,
I want to fix things,
I want to create things,
And I want to imagine the world with my creations.

Lily Dawes (11)

Macabre Manor

The clock struck noon at the dead of night,
Moans and cries, weeps and fright,

The ancient clock gave its last tick,
Those who died old, those who died sick,

All the bodies rose from the ground,
Even those who were beaten and bound,

Fire was burning in the pit of their sore eyes,
For everything they knew, were all lies,

Mischief, but wonder,
Falls, but thunder,

Lightning and rain,
Bliss, but pain,

All their life, they didn't know,
But now was their time to put on a show,

They had until the moon laid her head,
Until her face was tucked in bed,

The sun's cloak of light was folded away,
And so came the army that wanted to play,

They won't wait for you to blink,
Call for help, or even think,

Steer clear of Macabre Manor and the hills,
You'll never know the secrets under the daffodils,

Here is your warning, they will rise,
And then will come your early demise.

Abisha Jayan (13)

My Birthday Alphabet Poem

A is for age and
B is for boy,
C is for cake that we all can enjoy.
D is for decorations and
E is for exciting,
F is for fun, just like this writing.
G is for girl and
H is for happy birthday!
I is for ice cream, hip, hip hooray!
J is for jelly and
K is for kids,
L is for laughing, we're all eating like pigs.
M is for music,
N is for noise maker,
O is for my new orange music shaker.
P is for party,
Q is for queen,
R is for receive, I'll soon be sixteen.
S is for sweets,
T is for thank you,
U is for unicycle that was
V ery blue.
W is for wrapping,
X is for Xbox,

Y is for yo-yo on my new fluffy socks.
Z is for zoo. Happy birthday to you!

Calli-Mai Caulton (10)

The Great Forest

It is a wonderful place to visit,
Full of amazing creatures,
It is the forest.
The owl hoots at night.
Hoot! Hoot!
There are also many more creatures in the forest.
Deer run and jump and giggle all the way,
Bunnies leap all the way to hunt,
Flamingos dance around.
It is a great show.
There are also dancing competitions every day,
And the fish are the judges.
In the forest, there is a small pond,
Where fish swim around.
There are many more things.
In the forest, there are very protracted trees,
They look so fascinating in spring.
There are bushes that contain mellow strawberries and raspberries.
Horses are the best in the forest,
Because all the animals ride on them.
The cheetahs are the fastest,

So every day, all the cheetahs have a race and see who wins,
This is why the forest is the best place to visit!

Abisana Mohanathas (9)

This Is Me!

H appy as can be,
A mbitious in achieving my life goals.
P leasant as can be,
P erky and make people laugh.
Y es, that's me!

B right as the sun,
I nteresting as can be.
R eliable and always there for my friends and family.
T houghtful as can be.
H elpful to both young and old,
D ivine and strong in faith,
A ffectionate as can be,
Y es, that's me!

Y oung boy as I'm only 10,
O bedient as can be.
U plifting and full of hope,
N ice as can be,
G lad to be me!

W arm-hearted child,
R adiant as can be.
I nteresting and full of surprises,
T rustworthy as can be.
E njoyable to be around,
R eligious Christian boy,
S mart and sensible, that's me!

Lazzaro Pasquariello (10)

I Am A Reader

I am a reader
A dreamer of
Impossible things.
Of adventure,
And love,
And truth,
Of mystery and magic

But I am unsure
Which I love more
The words
On the page,
Or the stories that are spun
On the quills
Of the geniuses
Who taught me

To love,
To live,
And to be free

The people who taught me
The difference between
Good and bad
Between right and wrong

How to express myself
Through the words
My heart screams to be heard

These writers taught me
To look for those that will listen
To my truth
And to listen for those who won't

I see a world most don't
Full of all the hopes
Of the human race,
Of love
And joy,
And little things to smile about

I am a reader
But it is my turn now
To be the writer
For the people willing to listen,
For the next generation
Of people like me.

Jessica Elizabeth Miller (14)

Time Vs Childhood

The proof is in your changing face,
That time is flying by.
Past the days of those first teeth
And the endless question: "Why?"
But innocence still revives within,
Soft and pure and sweet.
As much a part of you
As the dimple on your cheek.

I hold onto these days so tight,
Before they slip out of hand.
Days of dirt and laughter,
Spent digging in the sand.
I try to keep my guard up,
To stop time from creeping in,
But it sneaks in while you're sleeping,
Which makes it hard to win.

I see those growing feet
And advancing words of which we speak.
The pants, somehow, too tight,
Did I forget to lock the door again?
Time must have slid in at night.

So, I fill my heart with memories
Like photos on a page,
Of daily moments passing by,
Snapshots of every stage.

Monika Shinh

Like The Moon Loves The Sun

Like the moon loves the sun
I want to be held like a mother holds her child
I want to be beautiful like the stars up above
I want to be free like a bird in the wild
I want to feel love...

I never show my thunderstorm of emotions
I keep the wars of my mind hidden
I stay up late wanting to make potions
And to my pain, I say good riddance

I tell the moon my darkest fears
He tells me about his brightest hopes
I lay in bed with tears
Wondering, how will I cope?

The walls are caving in
Yet, I push through it all
Day by day, I watch myself get thin
If only there was someone who would call

But once again, I'm left with my thoughts
Like the moon loves the sun
Your love will also run short
Until then, I'll enjoy our fun
Hoping your love grows stronger for the sun.

Fahira Mirza (14)

Life's Too Short

Life's too short,
Live life anew every day is what I say,
Let go of all the sorrows of yesterday,

Release any grasp of bitter feeling,
Time is the best at any healing,
From the sun's swift rise and setting,
There is no time for weeping or fretting,

So laugh with great heart,
Never let sadness tear you apart,
For life's too short for such a thing,
Always embrace what life can bring,

Love with no bounds,
All the way from the earthly grounds,
Till the hot, radiating sun,
Love till the 'morrow is done,
Engulfing us in its warm rays,
Until the very end of our days,

Every day is an extraordinary blessing,
So there is not a minute left for stressing,
Enjoy every last moment, no matter what has gone,
Always remember that life continues to go on.

Shaheer Sami (13)

Animals

Animals, animals, they're everywhere,
from incy ants to colossal bears.

Cheeky chimps laughing in the trees,
whilst something goes buzz, buzz which appears to be bees.

With a slurp and a bubble and the blink of an eye,
appears a hippo sinking in the mud, all disguised.

In the distance of trees, in my ear, I hear a roar!
I see a lion, in its mouth, I see something it's caught.

In my eye, oh my eye, I see,
hyenas giggling and laughing with glee.

Butterflies' colours shine in the sun,
whilst a bear wants some honey to fill its tum-tum.

When the glistening white moon comes out at night,
the wolves howl and give everyone a fright.

Oh animals, oh animals, we love them, we do,
one day, I will get one, maybe a dog or two.

Ruthie Forsythe (8)

What Makes A Poem, A Poem?

What makes a poem, a poem?
People have often wondered,
Yes, even the greatest have pondered,
That whether it's the wise use of language,
That's pulled together to create an image,
Or the clever way rhythm,
Formed to create a pattern,

That makes a poem, a poem.

Others think it's the feeling and emotion,
Conveyed in motion,
Or rather, the music that has been played,
With words that have obeyed,

That makes a poem, a poem.

People may believe it's how the poets use
Their playground,
And how their thoughts flow on
The merry-go-round.

That makes a poem, a poem.

But either way, I have only one thing to say,
That from the ancient word poises,
To the modern word poem,
It's meaning remains the same; to create.

Catherine Thomas (12)

Lady Of The Sea

I dance with the sunlight,
I fight with the cliff,
I'm ever so cold on some days,
Yet no one seems to think,
To swaddle me in blankets,
Or warm me by the fire,
Their faces yelp with joyous shock,
As they ride my back with glee,
No one thinks to ask me,
"How do you do?"
Or chats with me.
At night, I am a beauty,
Hold the souls of a thousand stars,
I skip with the moonlight,
And the whole night is ours,
He paints his milky glow,
Upon my icy back,
And we play all night long,
Until morning cracks,
Where again, I crumble cliffs,
And dance with the sun,
And I brood upon my troubles,
Until the day is done.

Megan Hawkins (12)

The Morning After

The morning after
I'm just trying to keep it inside
Nothing to do, except pray for a miracle
Gonna know another day
'Cause my feet are already up the stairwell
I heard you say yesterday
You've got to find your destination
This morning is all you're ever looking for
I heard the truth again
And the truth of a dream
I got a new level of confidence
I wasn't supposed to feel the pressure
Don't wanna let you get me down
And tonight I'm gonna do it the easy way
I'll let the past go and I ain't gonna stay
When I make my way
To say I'm sorry and walk away
And close the door and let you pass
I wonder what's wrong with you
When this world's gone
And you can always come back.

Rituparna Mishra (15)

Fly High, My Star

Shoulders down and back, my shining star.
Chin up, my beautiful star.
And place each foot forward, my hopeful star.
One foot in front of the other, my mesmerising star.
Have you got the rhythm, my stunning star?
Once you have, my enchanting star,
Raise your head and chin once again, my amazing star.
Look at all the people around you, my creative star.
Take a deep breath, my worldly star.
Maybe another, maybe two more, my lovely star.
And walk like you own the stage, my flying star.
Because now you do.
Spread your wings, my shooting star.
Soar into the clouds, my shooting star.
Display your inner beauty, my shooting star.
Find your happiness, my shooting star.
And most importantly,
Fly high, my star.

Farwa Khan (15)

Once Upon A Sky

The stars light up the night
The clouds so white, I can't bear the sight
The sun so gleaming, I love it when it's beaming
The birds singing, oh, the joy it is bringing
The plane as low as the skyscrapers
The trees that make the lovely nature
The flowers that blossom all year round
The birds that bring that lovely sound
Tu-whit tu-whoo, Tu-whit tu-whoo
Waking up in the morning, that is what I love to hear
The birds and the bees all so near
They bring me such lovely delight
I wish it would happen all through the night
The stars on the other hand, they sparkle in the sky
So far away, but feel so nearby
The moon so elegant, the sun says bye-bye
Watch out for the owls, goodbye, night-night.

Maisie Severn (10)

My Animal Poem

I love dogs and they love frogs.
I love cats and they love mats.

I love crocodiles and they play snap.
I love bats and the way they flap.

I love mice and they are small.
I love elephants and they are tall.

I love cheetahs and they are fast.
I love turtles and they are slow.

I love cows and they eat hay.
I love horses and they say neigh.

I love snakes and they say hiss.
I love dolphins and they kiss.

I love chimps and they are up high.
I love birds and they can fly.

I love sheep and they say baa.
I love tigers and they have hair.

I love hedgehogs and they have spikes.
I love zebras and they have stripes.

I love polar bears and they are white.
I love hyenas and they give me a fright.

Micah Forsythe (6)

Save Our Home

Us humans are very destructive,
We harm our beautiful planet.
Making Earth a victim of injustice,
But all we do is watch nature vanish.

Its consequences are very clear,
With wildfires and floods raging in places.
Icebergs melting, endangering polar bears,
It's time to make the right choices.

To stop this, we should start to recycle,
And also stop producing dangerous emissions.
By trying to travel by bus or cycle,
Make this your primary mission.

The world is a wondrous place,
However, because of our harmful actions,
It is perishing at a threatening pace,
So please stop your damaging interactions.

Ali Ghazi (12)

Aussie Animal Antics

If you happened to travel Down Under, just what would there be?
I'm about to tell you; starting at the great, blue sea.
You might see a tiny octopus with luminous blue rings,
A blue-ringed octopus; be careful, this thing stings!
If you travelled to the outback, you might observe a kangaroo,
Or maybe a wonderful wallaby (they have square-shaped poo).
There's also the koala bear that you might see,
They only eat the leaves from one particular gum tree.
In the rainforest, there are also splendid sugar gliders,
And in your back garden, plenty of spooky spiders!
So if you travelled down to Aussie, this is what there'd be,
Which did you like best, outstanding outback or spectacular sea?

Rebecca Morrison (8)

Seasonal Changes

I like to take long walks,
To the park in late March.
I love seeing all the flowers,
Dancing with the trees.
All the thick, long grass,
Swaying in the breeze

Summertime is here at last,
It's time to take a break.
But the summer will go by fast,
So I better make the most of it.
I go to the beach and swim in the sea,
And sadly, I got bit.

Autumn is now here,
It's time for a new school year.
The leaves on the trees,
Are slowly drifting down.
The ground is covered in leaves,
All red and orange and brown.

It's starting to get frosty,
It's beginning to snow a lot.
I go to the top of the hill,
And I slide all the way down.

I also make a snowman,
And it looks like a clown.

Patricia An (13)

Fantastic Fruit Party!

On a Friday night, all the fruit came out,
The first thing they did was scream and shout.
Let's have a dance party, let's have fun,
But only fruit is allowed to come.
At the party, there were...
Bananas doing the splits, watermelon waltz,
Tango mangoes, party peaches,
Popping and locking pineapples,
A DJ pear singing:
"Put your hands in the air,
Like you just don't care!"
Cha-cha cherries, blueberries boogie,
Raspberry rumba, Macarena melons,
Gangnam Style grapes,
And tap-dancing tangerines.
These fruit love to move and groove,
But the next morning, they were so tired,
They just snoozed.

Estella Thompson Oakley

Sweet Shop

I smell a sweet smell,
I wonder what it could be?
I look in the window,
To see a bunch of sweets waiting for me.

I walk inside,
I am overwhelmed with sweet smells,
I never know what to choose,
It takes me hours to decide.

Twirls, Flakes and Kit Kats too,
Don't forget about the jars too,
Maybe I could buy two jars,
And maybe a couple more chocolate bars.

I take out my money,
And clasp it in my hand,
I pay for the treats
And take the receipt from the cashier's hand.

Goodbye awesome sweet shop,
Until we meet again,
Maybe next week,
When I am back in town again.

Bethany Hoccom (13)

Animals Of The World

I'm going to talk to you,
About some facts about animals.
I'll start off with horses,
In fact, they are mammals.

Next, we'll talk about dogs,
There are many different breeds.
If you take them on a walk,
They'll be jumping in the leaves.

It's time to learn about birds,
They make nests in the trees.
When it gets too cold and frosty,
They'll fly overseas.

I've nearly done my job here,
Before I go, let's talk about humans.
We've been polluting the Earth,
And ruining God's creations.

Lastly, drive less and don't litter,
Don't cause any explosions.
Use water wisely and don't waste food,
Now it's time to think about our actions.

Joyce Chen (12)

King Of The Monsters

As it walks around,
You can hear its stomps loud and clear.
Stomp! Stomp! Stomp! Stomp!
Do you hear it?
Stomp! Stomp!
When it roars,
It sounds like the roar of a dragon
Mixed with a dinosaur's cry.
But when you see it near the beach,
You'll see its charcoal skin
And its majestic bulk.
You will also notice its snow-white dorsal fins,
In rows of three.
Do you hear sizzling?
Do you see the dorsal fins glowing blue?
That's it.
The city goes down as the beast fires
Its atomic breath from its mouth.
No wonder that it holds the title
King of the monsters!

Oskar Królak (13)

Seasons

Summer, a shining time of year,
When the trees are full of leaves,
And the grass is long.
The land is bright, warm and full of nature.
Autumn, an orangey, yellowy season,
With a gust of wind every now and then.
The floor painted in a blanket of leaves,
That fall elegantly from the trees.
Winter, a cold, mystical time for fun,
Snowball fights, snow angels and much, much more.
When Christmas is celebrated,
And woolly coats are everywhere.
Finally, spring, a newborn world,
With blossoming plants and baby animals.
Hibernation ends and the seasons' cycle is repeated,
Again and again and again.

Elena Mason (9)

Resplendent Triumph

When my blood burns golden with wealth,
When I defy the odds and emerge glorious,
When my title's on bookshelves,
When people think of me as victorious.

Desiring the hurt,
For it will make me stronger.
Because, one day, they'll look at me,
And what I've conquered.

Everybody who gave up,
Inflames me with determination.
My unstoppable ambition.
Because this is my definition, my decision, my mission.

Power behind the throne,
Until the impossible is achieved and
My name's eternally known.
And I've created my personal dreamland.

I'll do it for the glory,
Success is the theme of my story.
I'll do it to be a legend,
My life as a godsend.

Hannah Marie Bignell (12)

Summer Vs Winter

My favourite season is not summer but winter indeed
Summer is like a hot day on Mars
While winter is like a breeze
Also, get some hot chocolate
To warm you up!

I love winter because of the snow
Plus the snow also blows
Christmas also comes at that time, that is why I love the lights
People also like to skate on ice.

I dislike summer because of the weather
If there were less heatwaves, that would be better
One good thing is ice cream though
So I should say that summer is not that bad though.

I guess I like summer because of the food
So I shouldn't be in such a bad mood
And I love winter because of the weather
It looks like I like a bit of both.

John Segbefia

My Blind Love

Where my sight is in darkness, your voice brings me colour.
Your words carve out the world before me like a sculpture,
You are forever moulding, unfolding the Earth before my blackened eyes,
Allowing me to see.
My blindness cannot limit me to the dark,
When you fill my soul with so much light.
I will continue fighting this forever night with you by my side,
And though I have never seen your smile,
I have heard your laugh.
And though I have never seen your body,
I have felt your touch.
The only thing I have ever known is your rough fingertips against my own,
Your breath against my cheek,
As my skin shivers and yearns for your being,
To make me whole.

Jade Effemey (16)

Good?

Your smile
shines in the damned night -
And the sky
soars blue and white and grey and rainbow rays and they all look beautiful -
Then there are the times when I don't feel so incredibly lost because it's wonderful -
And there's the way letters stack in a certain order to create compliments and poems and art and I love yous and your name -
And there are those people who know what to say when you tell them something's wrong and they comfort you with the right words and too tight hugs and their strawberry-scented love -
And there are the songs that I adore
that are soft and sweet and quiet -
And - yeah, really it's not all bad.

Emily Hogg (16)

Who Cares If I Get Older?

Who cares if I get older?
If I celebrate alone?
If I fall closer to the end?

Who cares if I get older?
If no one else remembers?
If all else is underwhelmed?

Who cares if I get older?
If I am in an unassisted battle?
If it's all just an unaccompanied memory?

Who cares if I get older?
If I am exclusively inside my head?
If I am at a solo self-pity event?

Who cares if I get older?
If I am fumbling into dissociating?
If I am an isolated parade?

Who cares if I get older?
Even if I am hiding in solitary,
I will always care.

Kiera Ashton (16)

My Spoilt Pet

The other day, I adopted a pet
When I saw her, she was with a vet
I looked at her and said that's my pet
But only because when we first met
One was doing tricks on a table duvet
But on the other sheet, she was sitting down
On her face, there was a frown
I showed her a collar encrusted in diamonds
Her face lit up like a star in the sky
So bright, she was about to fly
I took her home in my car, then showed her a room
In the room were gigantic, pink, fluffy chairs
And some painted swans, there was a pair
Also, a brush for her lovely hair
The last thing there was a bear.

Ellie Jones (12)

The Generous Husky

H uge hearted dog, man's best friend and the friendship will never end. It's the husky!

U nhelpful? Say no! It helps you through the snow. It brings good joy and is such a good doggy. It's the husky!

S aving people from the cold, even if they're small. We must praise them for their brilliant outlook. It's the husky!

K ing of kindness, no selfishness. It has the righteousness to be king and is wise enough to trust. It's the husky!

Y outh doesn't matter to the husky itself because it is brave and helpful. It doesn't care what age it is. It's the husky!

Kavithan Davidprapakaran (8)

It's My Birthday

When I wake up in the morning, I know
That there is a new year ahead
I am one year older, so out I throw
Any sadness or woe, and jump out of bed.

Excitement tingles through my body
It makes me shiver, but then I grin,
Let's party, everybody,
My new year will begin!

It's my birthday, let's have some fun,
My eyes open wide in delight at all the gifts,
Let's cut the cake for everyone,
Forgotten is all the arguments and rifts.

Time flies on my birthday, more than ever before,
Evening comes, oh, I wish the day would be more,
I blow out the candles on my special cake
And I can't tell you what the wish is that I made.

Nawal Ali (13)

Artificial Reality

Dig further and deeper
But not more than a metre
They say they're believers
But deep inside, they are cheaters
Though there is greed guaranteed
We might plead
But we don't concede
We thought they revealed
But everything was concealed
We were set aside
As they were satisfied
Because the only thing we do is deny
But the more you deny
The more you don't even try
You made the generation cry
And refuse to testify
The truth isn't what it seems like
Though it may strike
It cannot psych.

Shaheera Kuchai (14)

Joy

The seasons are so bright,
When it's gone, we're all sad.
Animals and children play all day,
Parties go on for days.
Crowds seem everlasting,
Celebrating birthdays, anniversaries and more.
Having fun and sharing words,
Light shines there and here.
Music booms from unknown sources,
People dancing left and right,
Everyone having fun and playing.
The crisp crunch of leaves as people walk over the golden leaves of autumn,
The thin layer of white that covers the ground in winter.
The gleaming of the sun in summer,
The lambs eating the grass in spring,
Oh, it's so beautiful.

Richard Chen (11)

The Song Of The Forest

Lungs choking in the pure wind,
Trees, I feel you
Scared.

Forest, forest, crying for your life,
Crying for your kind, I knew
How we would use your dying:

Paper for our printers,
Space to breed our greed.

Leaves choking in the pure wind,
Trees, I heard you
Calling.

In the sea of the forest,
Trees, I heard you
Sobbing.

Sobbing to your kind.
We'll never let you be.
Instead of life, we choose:

Paper for our printers,
Space to breed our greed.

Victor Uzoma (10)

How I Had The Best Birthday Ever!

My name is Benjamin and I am 15 years old.
I celebrated my party when I was 14 in 2020.
Lots of people came over to visit me,
I was so happy.
People gave me money.
They were so generous because I didn't need toys.
I am now a big boy.
The awesome part of my birthday was that I had a yellow car cake.
It had candles. It was so nice.
I hope that I will be a better teenager and not make any mistakes and be a better person.
I am happy to be the kindest boy in the world!

Happy
Birthday
To
Me!

Benjamin Doeteh (15)

The Stars, The Waves And Me

I had a dream that is not at all a dream
One that is best of light and dark;
I am beside the lake and beneath the trees,
With a host of jewelled flowers;
Fluttering and dancing in the breeze,
What wealth had God blessed to me with archery?
As continuous as the stars above,
That twinkle on the Milky Way,
I dare to climb the sky,
I am free
I dance with the flowers in sprightly dance,
I have the jocund company of the waves,
I'll soon be the waves, the stars and the flowers,
Oh, thank God for archery!

Holly Hopkinson (12)

See

"Look up,
What do you see?"
"I see the sky."
"Yes, and?"
"The moon and the stars?"

"Look down,
What do you see?"
"I see the floor."
"Yes, and?"
"The grass and the soil?"

"Do you want to know what I see,
Through the blindness of my eyes?

I see joy and sorrow,
I see beauty; I see disguise,
I see suffering and happiness,
I see the wonder of life; I see regret,
I see tears,
I see smiles,
I see hope; I see unity,
I see our destiny.
I see you, and I celebrate."

Daisy Blacklock (12)

Bubbly Bob's Day

Bubbly Bob was about to get in the bubbly bath until...
He fell in the bubbly bath with his clothes on,
Bubbly Bob began to burst into tears
Then Bubbly Bob's owner came in
And picked him up and took Bubbly Bob to bed
Boom, bang, crash! Bubbly Bob needed to save the day.
Bubbly Bob saved a lizard called Squiggle Wiggle from falling
He blew a huge bubble and the lizard fell on it
Bubbly Bob was pretty famous
Everybody shouted out, "The brave Bubbly Bob saved the day again!"

Alicia Cocks

A Day With You

If I had a wish,
I'd go back to the days I miss.
When the sun warmed your skin,
And getting a tan counted as a win.
Or the breeze flowing through your hair,
And the trees waving their leaves through the air.
Even the snowflakes causing your smiles,
Making the freezing temperatures worthwhile.
And when we watched from afar,
As the moon outshone the star.
However, my one wish
Wouldn't count for a day I miss,
If you weren't there,
Enjoying the adventures we shared.

Jasmine Natasha Oakey (16)

My Little Brother!

My best day ever was when my little brother was born,
He had a smile on his face and would never yawn.
I loved it when he hugged me so tight and warm,
He would wander around when my dad was cutting the lawn.
He was the cutest person I had ever seen,
He would shout and cry to watch the screen.
Sitting in his chair, he would always lean,
I hated it when he screamed.
He played with my face all day long,
He would ask Alexa to play a song,
One of his most favourite games was ping-pong.

Dhyan Amith (8)

Finny The Odd Finned Fish

When I was 7, I got a fish
I kept him safe in a water dish
I fed him some food to keep him strong
But little did I know that all along
He was an incredibly strong fish
So I took him out of the water dish
I placed a bone next to his fin
And he threw it over to the bin
It soared above him in the air
Then I gave him my teddy bear
He did the same, I was amazed
This was a very unusual craze
My pet fish Finny is really the best
And he can do things better than the rest.

Ava Maconachie (12)

Birthday

H ave a special day
A nd enjoy your birthday
P arty all day till noon
P resents all waiting to be opened soon
Y ay! Hooray! Celebrating with people from different nations

B alloons and decorations
I 'm at home, partying all day
R eally excited to be celebrating this way
T his special occasion
H onoured to be taking part
D elightful moments to keep in your heart
A way from sadness
Y our special birthday with lots of love and happiness.

Alesha Sami (6)

Fun In The Sun!

At the seaside, you'll never feel blue,
Sharing smiles, you know are true.
Children giggling in the heat,
And young adults stomping to the beat.
In the cloudless, sapphire sky,
The shouting seagulls fly.
Stunning sandcastles all around,
With seashells that are now found.
The turquoise, shimmering sea,
That makes me crave iced tea.
And now finally, it's time for the sunset,
The stars will shine beautifully, I bet.
With a heavy sigh,
I'll wave goodbye.
If you read this, I love you,
And I hope you do too!

Aniqa Khan (9)

My Promise

Each day, I'll do my best
And I won't do any less
My work will always please me
And I won't accept a mess
I'll colour very carefully
My writing will be neat
And I will not be happy
Till my papers are complete
I'll always do my homework
And try my best in every test
I have fun doing sport
Rounders, netball and football
My favourite is gymnastics
Which I think is fantastic
I won't forget my promise
To do my very best.

Amy Liddell

My Voice

My voice is loud like a dog's woof,
And strong like a lion's roar.
My voice says *do-be-do* very often when I'm bored.
My voice goes loud when I shout at my sister when she has my stuff and when I sing with my friends.
My voice goes quiet when I talk to myself in my bedroom and when I'm whispering in the night.
My voice started when I was a baby,
And will always stick with me.
My voice wants to stop global warming,
And help people protect the bees.

Elizabeth Hurley (9)

Wild Dreams

Peace we achieve
By not doing anything crazy,
So why are my wild dreams
Unleashed every night.
It's different things
Like unicorns and tigers fighting,
So why don't I get peace in my dreams,
Like being the resolver of World War III
Or having a genie living with me?
Because the real world is a scary place
With dull, dark clouds high above me.
This should be my peace zone
And shouldn't be aggressive,
Where I'm safe and at peace.

Deakon Marcus (10)

What I Love About Young Writers

Young Writers inspires eager children across the country,
They use their dazzling website for children to have fun with poetry,
They also get growing children's minds working,
Maybe next time the poetry will be about rapping!
When I write poetry I see it in my head,
When I write poetry I dream about it when I go to bed,
Poetry keeps me cool, calm and collected,
Young Writers is the most supportive,
Young Writers is the best in the nation,
Come on everyone! Join us for the 30-year celebration!

Elysia Miller (9)

Stars

Up in the sky,
When it's time to say goodnight,
You can see something very, very bright.

But as you know, they are so, so bright that maybe,
They are brighter than your bedroom night light.

As the sun rises, it's time to say, "Goodbye stars!"
But no, they are coming at dusk with so many cars.

So now you see that stars don't disappear,
They're always there for you and me,
Even at dusk and dawn, you see.

Amelia Amirthaponkalan (8)

All About Me

I love pets,
But I don't have any pets,
If I had any pets,
I'd have to go to the vets,
I love all the beautiful trees,
I like a little breeze,
The sun is very hot,
I love having fun everywhere,
I am very kind,
I love to find things,
I have long hair,
My spinning chair is cool,
I wish I had a unicorn,
But I do have popcorn,
Going on a bike,
Is what I like,
I like fidget toys,
But I'm not a boy.

Natalia Szutenberg (9)

Tim The Bulky Dog

I have just got this dog and his name is Tim
He looks weird like he has been to the gym
He lifts weights over 100 kilos
I dress him up so he looks like a hero
He is big and a bulk
And his idol is Hulk
Sometimes, he stinks of beans
When he goes for a bath, he comes out green
He's very young, only one year old
And weirdly, his shoulders are very bald
That's my peculiar pet
Now I'm heading to the vet.

Charlie Nisbet (12)

Lockdown Life

When Covid started to multiply,
People started to die,
Our population was going down,
So then we started lockdown.

Children couldn't go to school,
So teachers started something cool,
They used an app called Zoom,
But as time went on, Covid brought doom.

Adults couldn't go to work,
Because Corona started to lurk,
But they started to go online,
A vaccine was finally made, but not on time.

Zoha Fathima (9)

Lockdown

I thought lockdown would never end,
Not able to see my friends,
All I'd do was watch TV,
But I really missed society.

However, lockdown had a good side to it,
That, I must admit,
Managed to pass my 11-Plus,
Learnt to be grateful for all my stuff.

Lockdown taught me to give my best,
Which helped me a lot,
But it had its ups and downs,
Like everything has got.

So before you say you hate lockdown,
Think of it twice,
And your opinion might flip around.

Tariq Konkobo (11)

Camping

I go camping every weekend,
Giving a helping hand to those who need it.
Never mind the midges,
You will get over it.
BBQ time, every night,
Staying up till midnight roasting marshmallows.
Going down to the woods,
Picking blackberries.
Pick the ones that are ripe,
You might get pricked by a thorn,
Well, that's not good.
Camping is fun,
Though take a look and see.

Kellsie Hindle (10)

Mother, I Love You

Spend time with your mother,
Before it's too late,
Stick by her side,
Like she did for you when you were a child,
Enjoy every moment with her,
Before you regret it.

Never forget the memories you have with your mother,
Or without them, life would be dull and boring.

And don't forget to say:
"Mother, I love you."
Before it's too late.

Ramondeep Singh Gahir Gaidhu (12)

Nocturnal Animals

Without any sound,
A sneaky fox comes prowling around,
Then comes a hedgehog making the bushes surrounding him rustle,
He is not in the mood to bustle.
Badger arrives, slowing his pace,
Hurrying is not the way he gets to places.
Argh! Oh, it's only a bat,
Swooping around like this and that.
Tu-whit tu-whoo, Owl's here,
Eating its prey from far and near.

Michelle Alenoghena (8)

Tonight, I See Stars

Tonight, I see stars,
Stars that look like chocolate bars!
I run all around, trying to fly,
Then I see a shooting star that's high.
I want to reach it,
But I know I can't.
Oh well, we don't need those stars now,
I can just make a wish and it'll be mine!
Amazing, glittery, delicious, beautiful, lovely,
Stars or bars, here I come,
Wherever you are!

Jaspinder Singh Kaur (11)

I'm A Ballerina Girl

I love to dance with my ballet shoes,
And I know some special, tricky moves.
I put my arms out and close my mouth,
So I don't shout.

I dance away on my small toes,
Like I'm in a superstar show.
The music is slow,
I just go with the flow,
Looking beautiful with a glow.

I use my legs,
Like strong washing pegs,
To hold me firmly up.
I stretch away each day,
That's my body, a star.

Arabella Pasquariello (7)

Sisters

Sisters are kind and also sweet,
They giggle when you tickle their feet!
They're sometimes fussy and also grumpy,
But give them a hug and they're snug.
Sometimes they fall out, but without a doubt,
They will get back together like a water spout.
They giggle and play for a night and a day!
Sisters are lucky and very snuggly.

Ivy Lucas (7) & Imogen Lucas (5)

Nostalgic Bullets

With youngsters causing trouble and having joy,
And adults coming out to say, "Oi!"
With teens and kids having a massive football game,
That could not be called a football game which is lame,
Because of various twists and turns,
The commentators and spectators learn,
To never ever underestimate talent,
That could quickly fade and burn.

Ezaan Ijaz (10)

Disneyland

Disneyland is amazing.
I got lollies there,
Lime-green lollies,
Frosty, lime-green lollies.
While I was licking my lollies,
I saw a rainbow.
I went on a treasure hunt.
I came first!
There were lots of flowers,
And chocolate buttons in the chest!
I told Mum how fun it was,
And went home.

Elizabeth Byrom (6)

Mountain And Beach

M ade over millions of years
O ver the rainbow to the sky
U nder the clouds
N ot always the same
T hey are always growing
A re really tall
I cy cold on the top
N ot always safe.

B ig, sandy area
E co-friendly
A re always sandy
C an be polluted
H igh tide.

Taaraz Siddiqui (6)

The Flying Cat

Two years ago, I bought a cat
I'm not going to lie, he was kind of fat
I fed him fish and tins of food
He thought that they were rather good
One day, in the dead of the night
My cat spread its wings and took flight
He soared above the clouds up high
And to my surprise, he waved goodbye!

Amerie Anderson

Books

B ooks are awesome, they can keep you entertained and interested.
O ur library is spectacular, full of colourful and exciting stories.
O n weekends, I discover new genres of books.
K ind of silly books can make you giggle.
S atisfying stories can make me relaxed.

Menaal Khan (8)

Imagine Dragon

Daytime's all normal,
Boring as ever,
Then when the sun goes down,
And the moon begins to rise,
My magic dragon opens his eyes.
He takes me where I want,
With no hesitation,
As long as I'm back before sunrise,
We can play forever,
And ever,
And ever.

Arli Mohammed

Lydia - My Best Friend

Lydia, you are my best friend.
You are so kind to me,
I enjoy your company.
You are funny and sweet,
Playing with you is such a treat.
We have been best friends since nursery,
I hope we stay friends for eternity.
I hope we stay in touch,
Because I love you so much.

Aqsa Kamran (5)

The Sky

Sometimes the sky is grey,
Sometimes the sky is black.
I like the sky most of all,
When it looks like the clouds are stacked.

It means a storm is on its way,
But very soon after, it goes away,
And we can spend the rest of the day,
In puddles, as we play.

Penelope Pickup (7)

Closer

We used to be scared,
That it would take some away,
In quarantine, we stayed,
And a bond, some have made.
Two years it has been,
Since it began,
I've aged, they've aged,
We've all aged, now you.
So a big happy birthday
From me to thee.

Sarah Uwadia (12)

My Tia Tia

My Tia Tia is so lazy
And also a little crazy
Tia Tia is so cute
She flaps about like a parachute
Tia is sassy and clever
We do lots of things together
She is so funny,
She makes me laugh all the time.
Tia Tia, I am so glad you are mine.

Alfie Trout (8)

As The Seasons Bloom

Long before the winter's cold
The bees guard their precious gold
The fields are rich with daisies and flowers
The sun is out before it showers
The snow falls like graceful flowers
The leaves curl and wait to grow
So let all the seasons be.

Fatimah Wahid (11)

The Things I Love

I love to eat lots of cake,
My favourite hobby is to bake.

I love to cook with my mum,
Eating ice cream with bubblegum.

Me and my dad love to train,
And we love to play lots of games.

My brother and I like to ride our bicycles,
And after, we enjoy our tasty popsicles.

Yousuf Kabir (5)

Spirit's Adventure

There was a horse called Spirit,
He ran so fast, he touched a train,
And it started to rain.
So Spirit ran to the woods,
And he saw a big-eyed owl.
Spirit looked up at the sky,
And saw a big, puffy cloud.

Rose Tobie (6)

When I Am At My Happiest

I am happiest when I am dancing, singing and writing,
I love watching Barbie and her positivity,
I can be anything I choose to be,
Taking part in sports, physical or mental like tennis, karate and chess,
I give them all my very best.

Zara Mehta

The Crab

Don't go near the crab,
It will snip and you'll cry.
It's very sneaky,
Just like a spy.
Ow! My nose!
It snipped my poor nose!
I think I learnt my lesson,
My aquarium should close.

Chidimma Mbah (7)

The Sound Of Winter

Winter, winter, I hear you coming
My spirit comes alive as you're here
The birds head south
As I head to the garden
And start the fun snowball fights
Let the fun begin!

Hajrah Bibi (10)

Butterflies

Caterpillars are childhood,
Butterflies are adulthood.
Just like caterpillars, not all of them are pretty.
But when the time comes,
We sprout into a magnificent butterfly!

Emmi John (14)

Lions Roaming Free

Lions roaming the land
Catching their prey
No escape
Because they are being watched
Trying to survive
To stay alive
That's what they do,
To stay alive.

Aaron Thomas Hindle (9)

One Wonderful World

One, one tree,
One, one bee,
One, one crab,
One, one scab,
One wonderful world,
And one me.

Henry Martin

Young Writers Information

We hope you have enjoyed reading this book – and that you will continue to in the coming years.

If you're the parent or family member of an enthusiastic poet or story writer, do visit our website **www.youngwriters.co.uk/subscribe** and sign up to receive news, competitions, writing challenges and tips, activities and much, much more! There's lots to keep budding writers motivated!

If you would like to order further copies of this book, or any of our other titles, then please give us a call or order via your online account.

Young Writers
Remus House
Coltsfoot Drive
Peterborough
PE2 9BF
(01733) 890066
info@youngwriters.co.uk

Join in the conversation!
Tips, news, giveaways and much more!

YoungWritersUK **YoungWritersCW** **youngwriterscw**